Robert Flanagan, "the kid," at 18 (1959)

OTHER BOOKS BY ROBERT FLANAGAN

FICTION
Maggot, a novel, 1971
Three Times Three, stories, 1977
Naked to Naked Goes, stories, 1986
Loving Power, stories, 1989

POETRY
Not for Dietrich Bonhoeffer, 1969
The Full Round, 1973
Once You Learn You Never Forget, 1978

PLAYS
Jupus Redeye, 1988

REPLY TO AN EVICTION NOTICE

SELECTED POEMS

*for David James,
in the pleasure of meeting you,
fellow poet, fellow Stafford
fan,   all best
          Bob*

ROBERT FLANAGAN

Robert Flanagan

27 August, 2009

BOTTOM DOG PRESS

HURON, OHIO
WORKING LIVES SERIES

Cover Photography: Nora Flanagan, Seven Hills Road
www.sevenhillsroad.com
Layout & Cover Design: Susanna Sharp-Schwacke
General Editor: Larry Smith
www.robertflanagan.com
rflanaga@columbus.rr.com

DEDICATION
For the women in my life, Katy, Anne and Nora

ACKNOWLEDGMENTS
The author gratefully acknowledges the publications and presses that previously published the poems in this collection.

PERIODICALS:
Ann Arbor Review: "Pennsylvania Dutch Country";
Artful Dodge: "Airway";
Beloit Poetry Journal: "The Open," "Window";
The Blackbird Circle: "Beached";
Contempora: "Parkman's End";

ACKNOWLEDGMENTS continued on page 94.

Contents

INTRODUCTION

Pugilistic ability is the one skill which begs for the attention of the reader more than any other theme in this collection of poems. It is the perceptive intelligence, it is the light and quick footwork of rhythm, tone and gracious footwork that recommends and grounds each poem and asks in the end: "How can we know the [boxer] from the [boxing]?" The sheer ability on display in Robert Flanagan's *Reply To An Eviction Notice* defies the accuracy of a single answer. We are drawn into these poems from different experiences, from different communities, from different avenues. It is simply not one single experience or one moment to which we can point, rather it is the experience in its entirety which requires the solid attention of the reader.

Pick any of the five section titles of this book, and one will notice immediately the lyrical footwork of a dancer/boxer:

> *To sink my feet past time in the Olentangy*
> *Everything rented, nothing owned*
> *When the ordinary came to light as jewels*
> *What we in innocence call our own*
> *Measured in part by life unearned*

It was hard for me to move from poem to poem, so I surrendered and let the poems do their necessary work. I began in "Indian Summer" with

> A white moon, white houses, white barns
> mercury lights pulsing like hearts

knowing that it was this light in all of its riveting colors that would radiate throughout this book. It would picture the "Cycle" of childhood by showing the reader:

> Our borough's slow boy
> late child of ancient farmers
> [with] . . . a slack grin
> on the moon of his face.

Flanagan dazzles the reader with the artifice of suspension and the water of disbelief in "The Swimmer." We are in a community of "Heroes" taking note of train collisions and an Italian sonnet that looks out of the "Window" of adolescence.

In the section *Everything rented, nothing owned* we are instantly confronted with the unexpected associations that lead one to unexpected revelations in "Murphy's Law."

"In Training A Man Talks To Himself" life is presented as a boxing match that not only needs support but requires encouragement. Observe:

> I will not let my body let me down
> cracking with fractures, my bones
> ——ribs, cheeks, hands——
> have been broken as often as any man's promises.

Read "Circus" which entertains this boxing theme as well. The title poem is in this section. It turns our attention to heritage and familial ties. It has the shape and feel of a sonnet but the footwork is decidedly different.

In the section *When the ordinary comes to light as jewels* we become aware of the poet's expert use of imagery and of William Carlos Williams dictum "No ideas, but the thing itself." Here we encounter reminiscences of past poets like: Whitman, William Stafford and the neglected Vachel Lindsey. All of these preoccupations are summed up in "This Too A Matter of Degree"

> That careless gesture walking home
> (Did I feel privileged by my poems?)
> plucking a sprig of forsythia
> in its fullness, dropping it casually.
> Ripeness is all. Zeus and Leda.

Do you hear the echoes of Shakespeare and Yeats?

The section titled *What we in our innocence call our own* focuses the reader's attention on Irish heritage in a variety of ways. "The Potato Eaters," "Kathleen Ni Houlihan," "Heirloom," "The Captain," and "Ghosts" all have and display a tone which addresses the affirmation of life. Memory is an acute part of this section as well. Witness "Memories of An Obedient Childhood," "Once My Father," and "Called Home," which guides the reader through the paraphernalia of the lives which occupy this Toledo community where:

> . . .All time
> and all life come down
> to a moment

where everything collides in a "Double Feature" that displays the themes of wit, dance and boxing :

> . . . the top dog hero
> was that yappy dancing dandy Jimmy
> Cagney, quick with his wit and fists
> a cocky little character who showed
> you didn't have to be the toughest
> guy around, just act like it.

A great deal of dexterity is to be found in the final section *Measured in part by life unearned* where everything culminates in the ease and simplicity of "Exchange Scholar," which is, in its totality, eleven haiku. I cannot break the spell by quoting a single passage.

It is the final knockout poem with its tight rhythmic footwork of 5,7,5 holding the flesh, bones and spirit of this poem together with white heat.

—Herbert Woodward Martin, University of Dayton

PART ONE

To sink my feet past time in the Olentangy

INDIAN SUMMER

A white moon, white houses, white barns,
mercury lights pulsing like hearts
and a mist hanging sweet as sleep
amid shocks of Indian corn.

Nobody moves about the pale farm yards.
Still as possums, houses await daylight:
barns groan with the weight
and ache of the dreams of animals.

I sink my feet past time in the Olentangy.
Scrub oak behind me give off a small noise.
Belonging to its shadow, an owl hoots
softly three times like an Iroquois.

CYCLE

Our borough's slow boy,
late child of ancient farmers,
swaddled in mittens and pea coat
pedals a gearless bike
though plowed, mounded snow
beside the highway. Skull
stitched and plated, he works
with a single mind, wheels
bucking and jamming, spokes
snow-clogged, as tractor trailers
swerve tracks about his sloped body
and his great Toltec head
bobbles, bobbles, a slack grin
on the moon of his face.

THE SWIMMER

Gliding long and easy
between strong, fluid strokes
(nipping air
from his collarbone's cup)
it's as if he could swim
forever, a water-beast
born to this, not foreign
as he is, exacting by artifice
suspension of his body
and the water's disbelief.

HEROES

Earlier he dreamed of becoming
great. Who doesn't?
Now he lives in the world. He packs
his own lunch days to save his wife
the trouble. Of three children,
each is his favorite. Eight hours
five week nights on the line
keeps the house waiting for him
as he eases his beater back along side streets.

Like bread dropping into a pool, spreading
and softening, he sits in the dark
on the front porch. Behind him
his family sleeps in their beds.
His eyes follow a wisp of smoke
rising. He imagines his town certain
as its stone heroes, dreams peace
for his children, stubs out his cigarette,
turns in.

Dew Drop Inn
for Chet Hazelton

Turning in on a whim
out of an eight year desert
and the noon sun, momentarily
blind in the aquamarine light,
I find the long bar in its same place,
along it the same faces
older, men on stools
alone with a drink,
here and there a secret smoke,
nodding to the old bull,
coughing at the old jokes,
sadder Budweiser;
down the line an open stool;
maybe the one I owned
for all those lost hours,
a noontime shot and beer
turned into night, a shot glass
dropped again and again
into a schooner, clink,
depth charge. Now,
my back to the door,
sunlight behind me,
I feel the blue cave before me
fill with the joy of time
denied: freedom
to let it all float past.

At the Scene of a Car Train Collision in Ottawa, Ohio

For years this boy had driven flat out
down the unbending northern Ohio roads,
past farmers gawking at him
from under straw brims;

nights, gone blind down narrow lanes
or come over blind hills at sixty-five
as if he'd catch what he was after
by speed or surprise.

Here is what led him on. Caught
broadside in town on a single track,
it spills into the street, runs suddenly
into a gutter, and will not come back.

Dropping In

Expecting a delivery of ordered goods
you open a door and he is there to say no,
he brought nothing with him.

His face is a stone blanked by wind,
eyes pocks of ice.
He speaks of owls

beating over snow stretches,
weasels' teeth clean of prey,
caves, silences.

Your house becomes a skin hut.
Beneath the floor's crust
is a pit too deep for light.

Huddled small for warmth, breath
too scant to cloud, limbs numb,
you wait.

A corner keeps you
through a months-long night. At last
he leaves without announcement, apology, your regret.

You open an eye
one lash at a time. Bit by bit
you begin the forgetting.

(owl
stone
cave)

The dark gives
onto a door—light—a world
capable of sun and green.

Looking back,
you see his place
occupied by emptiness.

STATE MESSAGE

The dozen clocks of this courthouse
reflect a dozen different times.
A thirteenth is heard, an erratic
clanging of tower chimes.

Above each clock I would place
a box to sound a voice:
This is chaos or local clarity—
citizen, it's your choice.

WINDOW

As a teenager I spent night after night driving
lead-footed through the plowed heart of Ohio,
in my father's truck going some other place
past dark farms, each with its white house
and a front window framing an easy chair
with the head of the family reading
or dozing in the lamp's warm oval.

Ten years of driving into tonight,
coming through the dark home to Ohio
and wife and children past white houses
still with a dreamt fear; the road turning,
the car slowing and now, inside, in the chair,
in the soft, eventual circle of defining light,
myself glancing up as the headlights flash past.

On River Road

The white egret
beside the Scioto
poised to strike—
on second look
a plastic sack
dangling in scrub,
though not for
that one moment.

PART TWO

Everything rented, nothing owned

MURPHY'S LAW
for Sheldon Gleisser

He never gets out of bed left foot first
nor tosses his hat on it,
nor puts red and white flowers together,

nor trims his nails on a Friday,
but always carries a rabbit's foot
and eats an apple a day.

Yet knocking on wood
his knuckles find
a fitting splinter.

Tossing salt over his shoulder
he blinds a waiter
whose father is the local judge.

Though he buries them in the moonlight
he fears the seven shards of his mirror
reflect seven times seven years bum luck.

Horseshoe in pocket
he steps around a standing ladder
to trip on a black cat.

Flat on the cracked walk
Murphy's looking over a five leaf clover
he's never overlooked before.

THE HEARING OF THE EAR

"I have heard of thee by the hearing of the ear..."
Job 42:5

I heard a voice I took to be God's
one time, damn lucky
to hear a thing over the stamp of machines
on our soot-bricked block where *job*
meant the swing shift, a hounding foreman
and pink slip fear.

Everything rented, nothing owned,
my dog choked dead on a fishbone,
my wife run off with some bush-league pinch-hitter,
I pitched my shovel at the coal pile.
"God damn it!
I can't live with this shit!"

And the sky stood still
but for a girder swung home on a boom. *Okay,*
that voice said. *Don't.*

THE CRICKET AT THE BP STATION IN EUREKA, MISSOURI

Whatever possessed him,
already sick or gone lame,
to abandon the patch of grass and brush
behind a service road off 44 West
and hop drunkenly about
an oil and gas stained map of concrete
under the otherworldly bright
floating arc lights
of a BP station
between a Taco Bell and the Olive Garden
where nothing green lives
and the night breathes
its poisons?
Whatever possessed him?

POWER

Schuykill County, Pennsylvania, 1870

Two men are here: a Welsh
night watchman assigned to patrol tool sheds;
a fired pitman, Irish.

This is their connection:
both are immigrants with families,
one bears a badge and truncheon,

the other, soot-black, stands stock-
still, back pressed flat to a wall.
His hands sweat, heart knots.

These pits send heat and light
into chandeliered homes
distanced by the bright

ambience of more than enough.
(From Mr. Gowan's Mt. Airy goes word to Coal
and Iron Police. "Get tough!"

and strikers' skulls are duly cracked,
men let go, and the Molly Maguires
organize to get theirs back.)

The watchman holds to check the time
beneath a gas lamp, pride
in punctuality his crime,

While queasy as a doubtful suitor
someone steps behind him
to offer a blue revolver.

The bent head flares—
blood a beacon lighting
workers to battle for a rightful share.

What remains?
A pool spreading the owners' assertion—
"The Irish are savages and must be tamed"—

one body in full extension,
the other, a runner,
sensing muzzles turning on him

yet still willing himself convinced
by Black Jack Kehoe and that shanty world
he has performed an act of political significance.

The widow is given whiskey
as witnesses vie for attention.
Neighbors shout up a party,

hound to earth
the winded assassin, and contrive
his roped, kicking death.

Having acted their part,
they turn home to bed, to sleep.
Their women lie unscreaming in the dark.

COAL MINER

for Annabel Thomas

To survive day to day
carving a livable hollow amid mountains
rising like debt over his family
he goes underground.

Skull sheathed in steel,
boots misshapen by mud,
he moves heavily.
Above him, a black sky.

The third eye of his beam
discovers a cone of dust.
The spongy bags of his lungs burden
his breathing like sacks of soft coal.

At times he can't help but think
underground thunder will crush him:
his skeleton a streak of lime
along the lignite grain.

Hauled up a shaft at day's end
he is released into air where sun
smolders under cloud slag
above a ridge of scar lift pines.

The mine's shadow hollows his cheeks,
deepens his eye sockets to pits.
He steps into the light. His eyes
glint like flecks of anthracite.

In Training a Man Talks to Himself

Sweat-suited, thirty-three, a journeyman,
I lumber a country road, a good distance
now into pain

snatching my breath like the hook
I saw start as a jab, then looked
again, flat on my back

as a white sleeve rose and fell
straight as a long-handled
sledge, my legs jerking like cattle

dumped on the meat house floor.
But I always get up. I can always take more
than any of them deliver.

Trial horse? Underdog? Shoulders hunched,
stunning the air with bursts of punches,
I punish my quitter legs, run

up the swell of a hill, exhaustion's edge,
and over, throw myself forward
like a handful of mud.

I will not let my body let me down.
Crackling with fractures, my bones
—ribs, cheeks, hands—

have been broken as often as any man's promises.
Somebody's talking here. It's my voice
winding the tapes of my injuries.

My Pop, club fighter,
was all the time yelling, "harder, faster!"
I'm hurting but I got to go a lot farther

yet. When I was a kid
what did I learn but "hit! hit!"
or else get licked?

Did he ever, just one time, say
Kid you got faults, but you do okay?
Anyway,

what in hell did he come to? A drunk
soaking up punches and his stinking gin.
He stuck out his mug and swung. I think

my man into mistakes, stick him,
pop, slip sideways, pop, feint,
let the sucker wind up and hit nothing

mostly. Double jab, sneak right lead,
set him to wondering, get him untracked,
then hit at the head behind the head—

like Scrapper Scarpati I nailed on the chin,
who got up after ten, grinned
like an idiot, sorry for being so dumb,

and got out of the ring and to his own bed
where he let himself go to what his brain called
sleep. Dead,

he keeps me company
each morning,
mute, just before me, mixing

with the shadow
a rising sun behind me throws
flat and sliding dark on the road,

a target for spit,
a stretched-out me, my own piece of night
waiting for me to catch it.

KNEES

hold magnets;
in the young, attract
cinders; later, other knees.

wear out trousers
and legs—fraying
like pulley belts.

bear up
man in woman's
bone-peaked valley.

are rocks
in the sacks of thighs,
clack together.

are good
city weapons, you don't need
a license to carry.

humble you;
bend but won't stretch,
prove you cousin to the ostrich.

BEACHED

In an orange feathered cap, the old goose
turns small eyes, green-glassed,
with pity on the girls
playing the beach boys' games
of tag and ball, dashing in the surf,
shrieking, their bleached hair flying
wild, confusing the body's speed
with freedom. She shucks off
a red cover-up and like a punctured float
sags rubbery-fleshed onto the sand
in a pink two piece, and rolls
hugely onto her back, beached.

Laughter washes over her like a wave,
as about her body's island strut
high-titted, bikinied teens,
backbones stiff with fears of youth.
Let Eve proffer her polished apples,
tart and juicy, she doesn't give a fig.
Adam's muscled, can pick his own fruit,
starve if he will. She owns herself;
has sloughed off Eve's pretty curse
and craves no attention but her own
and the sun's; lying spraddle-legged,
open to a heat deeper than Adam's.

REPLY TO AN EVICTION NOTICE

My mother and father camped in such apartments
in their time, landlord, promoter
of cramped endurances,
your rightful inheritance. Your father
purchased shrewdly and practiced ungiving
well. Mine did not.
So my sweaty bursts of living
are managed in rooms
gauged like parking meters, narrow as coin slots,
while from the landscaped, architect-designed
vantage of your home
the town lies before you a Monopoly board.
Ownership is your reward
and punishment; movement mine.

Semper Fi

In a bar in Delaware Ohio on November 10, the USMC birthday

Oh yeah, you were in the Corps?
See any action? A shooting war?

I had, I said. Oh yeah, where was that?
Toledo, mostly. Coupla times Detroit.

CURSE OF THE WEREWOLF

The terror of wino gypsies, you lunge
harried through Hollywood woods,
make-up on for so many takes
it seems *you* on the run.

Reel-long, the leading man
(with no more virtue than a razor-
shaven face, and your blond fiancé's favor)
tracks you down in rubber swamps.

snub-nose in hand, vow
in mind; he's out to kill. You
never chose this snarling; change
bit you unawares; but now,

too late, his wing-tips stand
beside your returning face.
The blonde winces, but will recover
and sleep comforted far from your disgrace.

The West: Field Notes

Buffalo: Pop. 216
A Consolidated Freight warning *Compressed Gas!*
rumbles past power line towers and railroad tracks
down two lanes of highway straight as a bullet
or Methodist preacher past wheat baked white
and poplars amazed in the wind's blast
to Town: a water tower, a church steeple,
a grain elevator huge as Ramses tomb.

Teapot Dome
The rolling high plains are oil.
All along Salt Creek rigs dip,
black as tar, insatiable as locusts;
bob like ducks in dark cool bars
where Warren Harding's good old boys
and friends of friends toast success.

Reservation
Single story square faded houses of Selish
look past chicken wire or unpainted pickets to foothills
grandfathers crossed to hunt buffalo, Blackfeet.

Cattle stretch necks beneath rails for roadside weeds,
a shack stands empty, blank windows the eyes of a drunk;
a '49 Pontiac, engine-gutted, flakes in the sun.

Bearing a boom-box on his shoulder,
a shock-headed teenager heads up the road to Moiese
where barb-wire marks the National Bison Range.

Inhabitants
Like a winded swimmer a crow crosses the sky,
stroke after stroke, beating to the shore
of a high pine knuckled into rock.
Cold wind trembles the branch.
The crow hangs on.

A cow skull turns up in a gully,
eye sockets like sea caves
scoured by tides to bleached white bone
where a spider throws a web,
settling in.

Medicine Wheel
On a Bighorn ridge a circle of stones
open to the sky invokes the unknown
for what lies beyond our understanding.

A cliff falls away like a ruined city
lost in the avalanche of history.
The answer the stones give is silence.

Overnight Camp in the Beartooths
Evening dulls a sunset to dried blood,
night stars burn as fierce as the eyes of Nez Perce.

A last spark gone,
the fire chokes on its ashes.

Pull a blanket over your head,
call it everyday.

GLOVES

From layered tables, I pick out
my size, work my fingers into sockets

warmed by fur turned,
a trapped rabbit, outside-in.

My hands' bones
become small skeletons;

fingers legs edging down a hole,
backed to a wall,

crouching into fists.
A fierceness like fear burns back along wrists,

arms, shoulders, to my heart.
I feel dark

like an eyelid sliding down, blood's heat
banked in the gut,

and hear wind whistling to gather
winter.

CIRCUS

for Wilbert "Skeeter" McClure

We stand, mastiff-stolid, as they wrap
our wrists and hands in leather-strapped
contrivances. Pride, hate
and hard hours sparring are to keep us
shaking off jabs of pity and fear, guard up,
hot to wallop home the lead-studded cestus.
Another slave, young cripple, opens a gate

and we blink into brassy glare, a bloody
circle of dirt, boxed-in,
two forms of blood and bone done up as men
to face each other with something near
grins the gaping take as sneers,
so caw approval: *Here comes some action!*
We are named enemies

—who in a more cordial country,
wisdom outstripping gaming war,
might knot cords of muscle over earth,
bear down a plow yoked oxen pull,
and evenings, cleansed, ungirdle
a melon-bellied, grape-nippled girl
and lay with her to father harmony;

men who might live
to stroll white-haired and oiled in delight
among the leathery-leaved green olives,
by Aphrodite granted life beyond these dead
legions croaking us on. We slog ahead,
square off in the stink of bears' guts,
chuck fists like hearts at one another's head.

THE OPEN

In memory of USMC Gunny Sgt. Bill Irving
& Staff Sgt. Ernie Temple

The Problem
Though their sergeants damn them
in skilled anger,
> *You want your ass shot off?*
> *Keep off the goddamned trail!*
stalking the wood line,
working swagger sticks against hard heads,
retraining the heart—still,
armed, grown men come like children,
wide-eyed, with shy sidelong steps
out of hanging shadow
into the open.

The Reason
For a man
will move without knowing
into thinning brush,
his straight line as if by the sun
warped to a curve:
> open spaces
> open spaces
are near; foretold
by a dry creek bed running
a weak stream of light through the vines,
a chest-wide recess to breathe in.

The Real Thing
Until it erupts—a geyser
of steam, white slivers of shock
and pain, a choking, then release
as fierce as a boy's wet dream;
though a dream all air, breathing
through a dozen holes,
with the light above, unlookably
bright, blinking in the spun blades
of the Medevac; then up, spinning
slowly on the long cord of his pain,
like a pale spider rising into the light.

PART THREE

When the ordinary came to light as jewels

Anna Babb with Crow-Black Hair

Hot as an oven,
cold as a clam:
you would compass these poles,
my small man?

Sleet of the heart,
the fire of milk:
a tunnel links the poles,
your worm trick.

THE ROCK TUMBLER
for Nora

Turning and turning in the limestone basement
between the gas furnace and the old coal chute,
the rock tumbler, its small red motor
Ferris-wheeling a black rubber barrel,

week after week grumbled in private,
rendering the rough and rocky smooth
like Demosthenes walking the windy shore
pronouncing stones, enunciating pebbles.

Amethyst, onyx, jasper, quartz—
souvenirs of Sanibel and the Beartooths,
a brass key, a silver dollar,
even driveway gravel

worked by time, water and grit
shone bright as the braces realigning your teeth
in the alchemy of your fourth grade year
when the ordinary came to light as jewels

in the bracelets and pendants
you meted out as Christmas gifts,
decades past. The hour
of that discovery lives in you still

(like an old lock-and-key diary keeping secret
jealousies, crushes, alliances, disputes
present in memory) as you explore
art as renewal,

the dynamo heart
forming livable truths,
reshaping the self in the mortal
tumble of time's rubble.

DOC'S GOT THE BLUES

for Gary "Doc" Holloway

Your horn sounds the lows
of memory, the hole
the guard you once were
tossed young thugs into.
Lock up. Cell blocks
holding con and C.O.
alike. All
backed to a wall
and being done by time.

Worn down by seventeen
years on the graveyard shift—
state job, right, but no gravy train,
where your breath was sustained by notes
sounded down those long night
halls, alto to soprano,
bawdy to dreamy,
hunting the key
out. Where now

you grin, saying *good gravy,*
man, it's all gravy now;
now it's all good.

WHILE I WAS DRIVING
for William Stafford

"When I was a boy he took me out and said 'Billy,
you watch that tree for a hawk,' pausing,
'You might see him before I do.'"

You told me that story of your father
and I felt for a moment I'd known one
like him, solid and kind—then
recognized it was in your poems
I knew him, and remembered with pain mine
staring out his room's window as if for rescue.

Your voice went on, near to me, yet
sounding distances between us wider than Kansas
or Ohio fields, those watercolor stretches
I tried to own by showing you.

"We worked together to build a house.
We did our best and he said it was good enough.
We lived there."

Speaking of him, you went far
into that world you carry from place to place
like a horseshoe scraped clean and kept for luck.

The wheel in my hands, the road drew us on
through my home state at sixty miles an hour.
I felt lost in that car.

FONDUE

for Scott Sommer

I try to skewer two chunks of raw meat
and the fork leaps into a third. My hand
quivers on the tines, its fingers
opening and closing like the mouth
of a dying walleye.

Meat in the pot of oil
gives off a smell of burning hair,
a mammoth screams away the click of silverware,
and my struck hand casts its shadow on the wall,
a cave painting.

ROADMASTER

On Christmas morning nineteen fifty three
your gift crowded the apartment living room—
more startling than a burglar, cherry bomb,
landlord or eviction. Its red tag reading *Patty*,

there stood a new Schwinn Roadmaster:
whitewalls, kick stand, coiled shocks,
chain guard, handlebars like steer horns, fenders—
all in black and white like your city blocks,

a gift your mother could not afford to buy
nor her twelve year old son dare ride.
Your sister's Kodak froze your smile
before the tree weighted down by tinsel.

Driven onto Toledo streets by your mother's pride,
you rode with eyes in the back of your head,
the bike as heavy as a banker's Packard,
its balloon tires rolling with slug-like speed.

To ride off the Irish blocks toward Dorr and Detroit,
the coloreds' turf, or the Italians' at Auburn and Monroe
was to chance Apache raiders like John Wayne's *Hondo*,
or cross the 38th parallel, a Saber Jet risking MiG bandits.

Spotting the enemy you stood on the pedals,
deaf to their shouts—*Hey boy, stop, we just wanna talk*,
pumping like a maniac, giving it more than your all
until behind you they tired and slowed to a walk,

screaming *Chickenshit Mick!*
Stopping to beg was as bad as being caught;
you'd seen kids whipped with their own bike
chains, held down as their spokes got kicked out.

You rode for your life all that year;
until, thirteen, out of breath and sick of fear,
you turned back to swing your uncle's night stick,
lumping a shine's skull, cracking a wop's beak;

Your gift more than a black and white bike:
To keep it you learned how to hate and fight.

PARKMAN'S END

"The old trouble in the head continues..."
Francis Parkman, letter to Dr. Mitchell, 5 November, 1883

His trail angled always back to Boston.
The chill drizzle of the Maine woods
a lifetime deep in his bones,
he gimped about the study in Jamaica Plain,
hot with disdain for Catholicism's hosts,
a half-century of conflict raging in his head.

An old man rowing the slow round pond
recalling the tumbling Megalloway, the wide Platte,
Reynal's squaw eating scorched hump, grease running
like wax down her brown fingers, he would will
destruction to the cottages on Lake George,
have moose standing gut-deep in tangled grasses.

Nights in his sleepless ache
he denied himself the ease of pining away
as would a Dacohtah, prey to visions.
He knew the beaver were beaver,
and would not call grandfather turtle or elk.
It was research drove him onto the savages' plain.

His belly a red coal, flesh shriveling,
he fixed his mind on Childe Harold
until the swelling dark was a grizzly
shot on the trail, surviving
to attack him again. He'd dreamt of bear
he whispered at the near edge of a silence

broken only by the shriek of a whistle
carved from the wing bone of an eagle.
A Ponka shakes a lance at black clouds
thick as buffalo. Lit by lightning
the struck brave sticks in the drawn brain,
lance tip a claw of sparks, body afire.

BEARS

Real ones are not enough:
camping, you imagine
rogues crossing land bridges, intently
approaching from ice floe and mountain.

On the trail—a stump,
twin to a cinnamon
bear, leaves you stunned.

By night there is danger
everywhere. Rocks grow hair,
garbage cans hunch in sullen hunger,
the shadow on the tent bares teeth.

Brush looming the clearing
crackles—something
bigger than raccoons is coming.

You dream polar bears silent as snow,
fangs longer than stalactites,
Kodiaks foraging for skunk cabbage roots,
mice, ground squirrels, and you.

It catches you in sleep—the final bear,
gargantuan, pitchfork-pawed, snorting fire,
wilder than heartbeats, the color of fear.

AN IDEA OF AN IDEA

I sit in a meadow of glacier lilies
at ease with my body, my legs resting.
An idea, like rising gas
trapped in hot lava of blood and flesh,
disturbs the flow. Slowly,
assuming the shape of a skull-top,
it puffs itself up.

          An idea of an idea—
from where? From bumping into country
and heating the body till vapors rise?
From where? Mind only these gases?
How can I insist on my self
as a willed act, when a bubble whispers
take what comes, become it to its limit,

pops, and is gone? Another swells still larger, reflects
the Beartooths bulking before me, rock and pine, gigantic,
undeniable as The Idea of The West—a surge outward
(millions dug into the eastern seaboard
like ants worrying a dying worm) from
narrow brick streets, institutions, proscriptions,
to a hard open peak, the bare rock of possibility

where snow hangs like a wave aching to break
silently under the sun into water
draining beneath the wind-carved shelf
a trickle washing down rocks,
a creek birthing trout, river silting fields,
The Mississippi, flatboats, steamboats, ports,
a town, Hannibal; a man, Mark Twain.

PICKING UP LINDSAY

Down a dirt road riddled with bumps,
byway for tractors or someone
off the highway looking for what could be there,
I pictured him standing with his oilskin bundle,
flop-hatted and dusty, a crackpot uncle,
his eye wild enough to brake my car.

Inside, he insisted on giving
entertainment; telling tales out of school,
of how he had walked the raw heartland planting beauty,
singing of Springfield, a magical city,
of Lincoln, St. Francis, Bryan, General Booth, all divine fools;
slept in straw, broke bread with whomever; this, his living.

Bread rhymes he called them, although
he sang silver ghosted visions like hymns;
drummed boldly fierce impolite unashamed gospels.
Rhymer and designer he called himself: Vachel.
What I know of that long prairie dream
I owe him.

On My Own Two Feet
for Noah Atticus Whitney

this trick, new, would amaze!
I lift on my toes, sway back on my heels,
bend, pivot, stretch, jump
for no more reason than feeling
a phrase reel along muscles,
each act speaking memories.

(From a knuckling shuffle, heavy-skulled,
a furred man rises. Such heights!
Sky's vacuum draws out a dream, a bird-god
striding the air. Earth beneath him
barely holds him at his feet. Stumbling,
he will grab it, but differently.)

A pelvic basin gives me a precarious balance
(he will learn to think this act and call it grace).
A neck keeps my head high (he will call this pride).
Mud plastered on a bone frame, a clever doll
—look at it, rattling and shuffling, loose,
grinning, dance (he will call this joy) upright!

WHITMAN'S SONG

When they tried to catch (to identify and tag) it in clever pens
it rattled and banged, escaped as you on your bed, cagey,
misered one last secret (Traubel scribbling and scribbling), launched
diversionary south and west a troop of wild imaginary bastards.

You and your self, bodied airs, hugged tight, frightened
boys on a raft. When the storm broke, lungs, song-bubbles, collapsed.
Your singing had no more meaning than wind in from the sea—

less for the curious (the Professor of Gross Morbid Anatomy dissecting)
tracking you down to your last known address.

News from a Backward State
for Colette Inez

Pragmatic researchers have established a base
among us. We are trying to invent
the automobile, they believe.
They think in secret
our kind must be developing
locomotives. Now that they are here to observe,
they tell us, it's only a matter of time
before they discover our chariots.

One aims a microphone at my head,
another a video camera, a third spills
into my hand a strand of bright beads.
"We want the truth. We know
there must be more going on here."
They point to a dark hole in the hillside.
"Isn't one of your people up there
Working on the wheel?"

PENNSYLVANIA DUTCH COUNTRY

lies beyond the thru-way
Gift Haus selling souvenir
hex signs and shoo fly pie,

where air is so rich
it erupts into trees, dripping
dark trunks to root in darker soil;

where vast oak and stone barns
in fields below the running humps of hills
sprout like monstrous pumpkins;

where citizens of stone towns
in dark suits and dresses gather at church
to come to life in scripture;

where boys playing baseball in pastures
wear wide-brimmed black hats and suspenders
like ancients shriveled with age.

THIS TOO A MATTER OF DEGREE

That careless gesture walking home
(did I feel privileged by my poems?)
plucking a sprig of forsythia
in its fullness, dropping it casually.
Ripeness is all. Zeus and Leda.

Part Four

What we in innocence call our own

THE POTATO EATERS
Ireland, 1847

The raw potatoes
fit their fists like stones
picked to chink walls
banking layered sand and seaweed
as soil against wind's emptying.

After weeks of strangling on thistles
and grass, bushels of stored seed
praties seem red stones
yellow stubs of teeth can bite;
appear miraculous:

The Miracle of the Stones
whose fevered believers,
the skin and bones of one family,
hunch in the flush and stinging fumes
a turf fire gives the low cottage,

eating their acre and two roods.
Eyes, tearing, bug from sockets,
cheekbones jut like stones
from peat-dark undersucking hollows,
sickle-curved backs

fray with smoke, and faces
smolder like banked coals
in the heat of sudden feeding.
Seasons to come are wind on stone
now. Gums and the odd tooth work

pulp, skin, and eyes
though skulls keen visions of stone fields,
seedless. They suck from fingers
now a thin ammoniac juice,
the taste of turf, of earth.

Kathleen Ni Houlihan

Black shawl binding
her pinched, bone-white face,
the old woman is knotted
double by hunger's drawstring.

On a road a young Irelander
sprawls, broken, another
mother's son lost
to a nation's hatred.

Kneeling to him like a lover,
she cradles the bloodied head.
Dry lips brush a cheek;
yellowed teeth tear into meat.

HEIRLOOM
for Maury Collins

The caprice of the strokes
caught here in time's hardening as a stray
bristle visible just beneath the paint's gloss
like a single hair of an ice-locked mammoth;
the sooty, chipped blue,
a yellowed white beneath it streaked in cracks
weak as a senile grin:
whoever tried to brighten this monstrous chest
a second time, knew failure, hid it
in the basement of the old house
and is forgotten.

We take it in as ours,
stripping and sanding away paint
layers, blue, white, and surprise
into walnut, the strong dark grain
revived beneath the pressured circling
of our hands, like the ghostly
image of a great-grandfather
buried long before our birth,
represented in a retouched tintype
centered in the reclining circle of his family
at what seems a outing, dancing
on the old sod what seems a hornpipe;
or one of him seated white-collared in dignity,
mustache waxed heavily as the walnut breakfront
behind him a dull gleaming.

Our hands complete their circles, though
we are full of aches. This dulling work
is redeemed by the use, more than worth,
of the chest. Restored, it will hold
what we in innocence call our own.

THE CAPTAIN

My father's father was the Captain:
six foot two, two hundred ten pounds,
red neck like a stone porch pillar,
an honest cop who kept his house,
wife, four sons and one bloodhound
under tight rule and in strict order.

Blue uniform pressed, buttons shined,
his hardwood billy waxed to gleaming,
the Captain's creed was simple: a place
for everything and everything in its place.
He'd bet that blindfolded he could find
anything in his room and he never lost.

At the long oak table beneath the crest
Certavi et vici O'Flannagain,
smelling of talcum, red mustache waxed,
the Captain sagged. His face came to rest
in a plate of beef and boiled potatoes,
the fine red hair matting with gravy.

A parade uniform over his stiff flesh,
he went home in good order; ages past.
The Captain: white dry bones
A silver badge, eight brass buttons.

GHOSTS

"In the privacy of our thoughts, at least, we really occupy quite different dimensions and some of us are walking like ghosts through the world of the past." —Loren Eiseley

Restless, walking known streets
late in the home town's silence,
I see him! He comes solidly
toward me, striding his beat,
young, ruddy, the recalled eyes blue,
a uniformed patrolman, heels clicking,
billy held lightly behind his back
looped to a wrist with a leather strap.

Does he feel my nearness? An unease
like a cloud covering the moon?
He shrugs. Ending his shift
he goes shadowed to his home,
bride, bed, engendered sons,
and a grandson, last of the line,
who stands in a joined dream
seeing the light go out.

MEMORIES OF AN OBEDIENT CHILDHOOD

My father in his scar-tissued wisdom
warned me never to walk away from a fight.
My mother, her thin lips tight,
believed each sin had its instant of choice.

My father, urging me to get ahead,
recounted the lives of Carnegie and Ford.
Greed was the worst sin: Charity
the chief virtue, my mother said.

Fixed in my dreams my father prods
from under the old Dodge he kept running somehow.
My mother peels potatoes at the sink,
cautions my life with one cocked eyebrow.

ONCE MY FATHER,

between wars, between hospitals,
sat down with me, his hands steady,
and played a day away
at checkers at the kitchen table.

As in home-front rationing
when copper takes on the glint of gold
I horde that memory like a shining
scrap of foil, hoping to form a ball

big enough to seem a world.

CALLED HOME

I come awake in my mother's bed
alone, before bird song, and hear
the timpani of all night garbage
crews rounding up the discarded.

Is she awake now? Somewhere
A rooster puffs himself up,
brazens a promise—in the city?
Hope? Or did I hear that, really?

Does she hear it? Behind glass
walls, pills, mask, through tubes
netting her life as she lies,
hands lightly across her chest,

listening to her heart perhaps
or, deeper, hearing the fault
in the bone, the wearing away?
Does she hear it? Slowly,

the lid of a moonless night
cracks. Light leaks through
as pale and chill as my sweat.
About me in unexpected disarray—

the paraphernalia of another's life,
like supplies for an exploration
or horde against famine.
My body trembles,

a wire carrying a message
and shaken by its power.
Studying my hands, each scar
tells some aim come untrue.

So many times I ribbed her
about her visits—the way
she would rise on the last day
and pack a bag at four a.m.

Kidding was our manner.
No need for honed words
slicing to the heart of the matter;
we took the real for granted.

I hear my father now, sleepless,
eyes gauzed by cataracts,
brain strangling on air,
rummaging the unfixed apartment.

"She'll be all right, won't she?"
he asks time and again, opening
desk, bureau, cupboard, chest,
hunting for the nineteen twenties

when in muscled pride
he is carrying his bride to bed,
driven by blood's history
to release the impending seed.

Now she lies in a strange room;
figures of nurses (like angels
or ghosts?) float the white halls.
Does she pretend she is only visiting?

On the screen of the bedroom window
sparrows scallop the dawn sky;
the purple ikon of a grackle
crosses my view, and I allow

the night's dream to return.
I am walking from the cave of myself,
buttery trumpets of daffodils
at my feet, the sky sun-filled,

and come unstuck from earth,
breathless in soul's bloom,
to enter the bright air—
before waking to her room.

As a boy here I heard, soundly
anchoring the world each morning
and evening, church bells, and our family
planned the future with indulgence.

That was when everyone lived forever,
before any one life became a question
without answer. She is the question
now. What will she accept? Or how?

As a prayer last night I said all
I could: a whisper to that weight
pressing dinosaurs and posies to coal
to please rest easy on her bones.

Is she too mesmerized by darkness
like a child at the lip of a well?
Or fully expecting light to reveal
a trap door to an attic room

full of treats, empty of hurts?
I force my body to lie still,
hands on my chest. My heart
beats down into an opening.

At bottom, what is real?
The conjured future, the after,
our memories of a lost past?
Or solely what we feel,

the pump of a singular pulse,
the breath that, once gone,
never returns? All time
and all life come down

to a moment. This
is the only lifetime ever.
We are in it as in sun between
clouds. As now I enter

a space with no name
where, waiting, I am
not father, mother or son
but all, the one.

After Him

Nothing impairs the symbol that's true;
be it from houses, be it from graves,
let him praise bracelet, pitcher and ring.
                                —*Rainer Maria Rilke*

In my father's bedroom
time has turned to after him.
Within his children's flesh,
his bed shrinks to a bed,
his clothing to clothing,
his chest to a chest.

I hear amid talcum smell,
suits hung draped with plastic bags,
note pad scribbled in red ink (get oil
changed, storm windows in), check stubs,
news clippings, snapshots, balls of string,

a stopped pocket watch,
my father's whispering:
Memorize me. Pass me on.

FOR BIRDS

Born beside an aviary,
our first child's talk
began as crow *caaas.*
Now three, she flies
about the yard
while her sister tries
to escape her walker,
flapping her arms
like a frantic gull.

With our care
and watching outward
we help them choose
the flight we made,
teach them to use
wings to accept the air,
and this picked branch,
the wide sky's root,
for jumping off.

What strange birds we seem!
Sheltering from cats and wind
in a nest all openings.

THE GARDEN, THE CHILDREN

Dirt where I promise beans and corn,
you ask when they will come.
I tell you what I can:
These things take time.

Your mother has cried in pain
from childhood scars and, given nature,
from memories of your future.
The beans need rain.

Blood-dark, I at times become
a man to fear, the stranger
who masks fear with anger.
The corn needs sun.

Safe for now from flood or drought,
We stand by our measured plot.
Children...
Sun. Rain. And time.

ONCE YOU LEARN YOU NEVER FORGET
for Anne

Fated by a birthday, my daughter
straddles her present down the drive,
small arms fret tight enough
to break a father's silence:
"Will you *listen*? Relax!"

With tangled, prickly bushes
one side, hard dirt
the other? Fall after fall
peels knees and elbows to reveal
blood as her body's secret.

I tell her it's the only way
she'll learn, and find myself
the ogre in a nightmare
I escaped. We should escape
pain, the child's heart tells us;

yet I expect her to believe
pain is growth? I learned that
a hard, backhanded way:
*You'll thank me later, boy,
When you're a man.*

What should I enforce now,
and why? I want to spare her
the traitorously narrow
wheels that keep angling
to home in on hurt:

I want to carry her inside,
It's all right, all right,
keep her the princess no one
frees to a world of cinders
and roads with no white lines.

Pain learns my nerve ends
all over again with her.
I remember. I never forgot.
Yet my feet refuse
To give up their place.

She crashes. "Better," I say,
"Try again." And witness
fear winging her shoulders
as she wobbles away from me,
as we balance the best we can.

Spam

We fried it in a blackened pan
over a fire of dead branches
in a ring of rocks and ate it
with hard-fried eggs and fried bread
garnished by stray pine needles
that we warned you not to eat
in our camp below the Beartooths,
the second-hand wall tent all
mildewed heavy green canvas
held up by enough poles and ropes
to rig a sloop.
               We were still
young then, your mother and I,
seeing life ahead as bright
as the sunrise that chill morning,
the two of us with our tin cups
of steaming coffee, and you
two girls, little red riding
hoods up on your new sweatshirts,
mopping dented tin plates with toast
just as we told you to do,
passing on what we had been taught.

AFTER THE DIAGNOSIS
for Quinn Flanagan Whitney

Being driven home
along the river road
by my daughter,
sitting in back
with my grandson
strapped in his car seat

I hear a long low whistle
beyond a screen of trees
and my grandson, four,
starts up. *A train!*
But we can't see it,
I say. *It's in the distance.*

At the edge of town
we're stopped by a gate
and flashing red lights
as a freight rumbles past.
Papa, my grandson says,
We're in the distance.

DOUBLE FEATURE

Garfield, that soulful Hebrew hood,
rolling his boxer's shoulders and turning
his sad Jesus eyes on the two-faced blonde;
and the stiff-lipped lisping private dick
Bogart in dark fedora and dark suit,
skeletal but for the shoulder holstered
weight of a black gat in his armpit,
they were our heroes, the balcony pack
at Toledo's Avalon theater
flipping straight pin-spiked candy Dots
at square kids beneath us and fronting
the pimply ushers, telling them to button it:
they had to get home after work
and we knew where they lived;

but for me, the top dog hero
was that yappy dancing dandy Jimmy
Cagney, quick with his wit and fists,
a cocky little character who showed
you didn't have to be the toughest
guy around, just act like it
often enough that people believed it
and sometimes even you did;
a lot like it was with my dad,
a world war vet with the purple heart
and fire-haired ex-lightweight club fighter
who'd once juggled balls, clubs and knives
while walking a free-standing ladder
in vaudeville's dying days; he

was a little guy, even next to me,
and the spitting image of Cagney
people said, with his snappy patter
and scrappy banty rooster temper;
"So," he'd say, "Micks are all talk?"
standing over some mouthy wisenheimer
who now kept his cracked jaw shut. All
through my teens I saw Dad and Cagney
as leads in my own private movies,
and took comfort in how thin the line
between Hollywood star and local loser;
only when he'd been gone for some time
did I see how all along it was Dad and me
paired in the double feature of our lives.

PART FIVE

Measured in part by life unearned

ATLAS

Lost in Oregon, hunting my bearings,
I open a road atlas, turning
accidentally as a birthplace to Ohio,
Toledo inset in an upper corner,
to discover again Detroit
and Monroe, the main thoroughfares
red Xed like crosshairs
over the city's glass heart

and I sight as if through a scope
down years, past miles, to that point
in a boy's four-cornered world
where a railway apartment was
escape and prison. Summer heat
held nights by a flat tar roof
bore him to the living room floor.
On a mattress pad beneath open windows

he watched in the dark until sleep
fabulous long-haul tractor trailers
lit like beacons in the empty streets
idling hugely, vibrant, at the corner
waiting for the green to bear away
their burden of goods, going into
on eighteen singing eight-ply tires
an imaginable expanse of headlighted dark

twenty years past. Here,
studying the map of a city
as lost to me as Atlantis, I see
for the first recognizable time
beyond the hometown's corporate
limits, the crux of my youth,
those cross roads opening out
to become interstate routes.

EXCHANGE SCHOLAR

Here to teach haiku,
Sato from Tokyo puffs smoke
from a Lucky Strike

over beer and shots
at an off-campus gin mill,
and levels with me:

hard boiled crime stories,
not haiku, are his true love
and he stays up nights

in his rented room
smoking in bed and reading
Hammett and Chandler—

like the Lonely Wolf
private detective. He says
he can tell me this

because I am not
like the other professors,
not the college man,

more the real McCoy
American street-wise guy.
I shrug my shoulders,

another life, that;
one I'm glad to leave behind.
But he looks away,

so I tell him how
on a bad night in a bar
back in Toledo

I pulled a snub-nose
Smith & Wesson .38
on some big mouth punk.

Ah, Toredo guys ,
he says, like Flank Sinatra
and his pack of rats.

HEAT LIGHTNING

It's been building
to this all afternoon.
Without words
we knew it,
sprawled in the yard
in a swelter of sun,
then under loitering clouds
thick and impatient.

Gathering the blanket,
your dark hair kept
from falling free
by a triangle of pink,
you mount the hill to the house,
and I hear in the swish of flesh,
thigh on thigh, the heat
you have drawn from the sun.

In the room's dark
we are searching
as the window fires white.
Heat lightning.
A welter of rain begins
and the storm breaks fully open.
In white flashes of heat
We find and know each other.

GET TOGETHER

for Mike Harrah, Tom Ireland and Tony Kretowicz

You left hot-rodding a coon-tailed Ford
as if into orbit; now drawn
by years and the old town's lure
you haul your body home
to the railed front porch to wait

for friends of the child you were.
On their own trail, having lost
some part of themselves, they wheel
down the old street in chairs,
dangle between sticks, come tapping.

They have come for a touch.
What can you spare?

Birthday in the Mountains

Having climbed through a daylong light
celebrating a birth

we hole up, curled
on a dark ledge above our world,

and like our lives, join
two single bags to keep us warm.

My breath snags white in your hair,
drifts loose, disappears in thin air

as I hold you tight,
watching over us stars arc toward midnight,

a beginning and an end
where your life realizes yet another descent.

It comes. You are sleeping. The round
of your breast teaches that shape to my hand.

FOR MY WIFE, HER GREEN EYES AND THUMB

If nightmare assassins hunt me
down, chopping off head and limbs,
this woman would plant my remains,
the butchered trunk, in the potted jungle
of our life, watch over me with green eyes
and thumb, water me, set me out in the sun,
turning me with earth's turning, so that in light,
heat and air, tended, salvaged—by heaven
I might sprout back to life like a banyan,
knotted roots, waxy leaves, fleshy figs,
as she becomes a fluttering of sun-
lit feathers, and alights to nest,
eyes closed, kindling eggs.

DIRECTION

for Kathleen Rose

The radio crackled that day I drove
a road ending where you waited.
A tornado met me halfway, aimed
anywhere, wild, uprooting: the sky
blackened, the river ran backward,
my old car shook, beached on gravel,
the world held its breath one lifetime—

then rain cleared the way and (years
saved, distances, recognitions,
marriage, children, a home,
tonight together in a warm room
joined by a habit of love
measured in part by life
unearned) I headed toward you.

GOLDEN

Within an embracing dark
we learn a gentler, slower art,
matching the beat of two hearts;

in what an apprentice terms decline
shaping for ourselves, like Rodin,
the soul's image in our hands.

BLOOD IN THE WATER

So this is what it's come to
after youth's big talk,
another old man in pain
grunting *uh-huh* when the tech
asks if you're doing okay
as the surgeon grinds down bone,
and stitches shut the bloody hole
left by the broken molar:
you swallowing blood—
Rinse. Spit.
—and damn fool that you are
missing the old days when
mouth stuffed with gum rubber,
blood pouring from your nose
and, swallowed, souring your gut,
you stood up to the punches
and gave as good as you got,
proud of not giving in
then; still.

AIRWAY

for Mona Mary

Or breezeway the landlord called it,
in telling our folks why our apartment
ran seven bucks more a month than the others,
except for the McManns' next door to us,

even if we never felt anything
you could call a real breeze from it.
Still, it held air, as in an open tank,
making it easier to breathe in the city heat,

meaning we were the lucky ones,
the McManns and the Flanagans,
in that row of chipped brick second story flats,
as we each had a window opening

onto a five foot wide patch of cracked tar
open to the sky, with metal vents sticking up
from Maloney's bar below and a rust-scarred
tub left by a lucky or evicted tenant before us.

With Mom at work and Dad sick in bed
our place was quiet, but not the McManns'.
Mr. and Mrs. and their five girls, mad
or happy, made noise day and night

and my sister and I watched their place
as if our side window was the television set
we didn't have, or the movie screen
at our Monroe street theater the Avalon.

Mrs. would walk past curtainless
windows in a slip, big breasts flopping,
and one time when Mr. came home drunk
she cold-cocked him with an alarm clock

thrown overhand as hard as a fastball
by long Gene Conley, Toledo's ace,
pitching his team to first place
over Louisville in the pennant stretch.

Though there was one summer when, sober,
Mr. held a job and Mrs. wore clean dresses
and on hot days carried white china pitchers
of water to pour into the scrubbed tub,

and the swarm of apartment kids,
fat and skinny little boys and girls in grayed,
frayed underpants, few girls bothering to hide
the new little nippled bumps on their chests,

splashed and shrieked in the iron, claw-footed
pool, and on some evenings even over our noise
you could hear breaking waves of cheers
from Swayne Field, the green walled park catty corner

to us on Detroit where the Mud Hens played,
and if you popped out of the tub and walked
near naked and dripping wet to the airway's end,
you could see lights bright as stars come to earth.

ABOUT THE AUTHOR

Robert Flanagan was born in Toledo, Ohio, where his family lived in a railway apartment above a bar at the corner of Monroe Street and Detroit Avenue. His father was a disabled American veteran, a U.S. Marine who'd seen combat in France in WWI, his mother worked second shift at Champion Spark Plug, and his sister Mona, ten years his senior, was an aspiring artist. "As a boy I sat on phone books on bar stools watching the *Gillette Friday Night Fights* and *Pabst Blue Ribbon Fight of the Week* on TV with my father. It made me a die-hard fan of the sweet science, taught me that a tactician like Archie Moore could be as formal and poetic as Yeats, and led me in my teens to try my hand(s) at the sport with retina-detaching unsuccess."

Schooled at St. Ann's grade school and Central Catholic High School in Toledo, he later worked as a dishwasher, night watchman, and janitor before joining the U.S. Marine Corps Reserve where he served as Corporal E-4 in a Recon Battalion.

Although neither of his parents had completed grade school, he enrolled at the University of Toledo, studying philosophy, literature and theatre, and discovering there his love of writing—poetry, fiction, plays, screenplays, comedy routines...At the University of Chicago he studied under novelist Richard Stern and poet Elder Olsen, and worked briefly as an associate editor at the *Chicago Review*. To fund his education, he worked in Toledo as a day laborer, night campus police dispatcher, cafeteria line worker, and city weed-mower operator, and in Chicago as a dietary orderly and a psychiatric orderly at the University clinics, and a social caseworker for the Cook County welfare department.

Flanagan has published a novel, three collections of short stories, five chapbooks of poetry, as well as essays and reviews. He has had two stage plays produced professionally and two screenplays produced as independent films. Retired as director of creative writing at Ohio Wesleyan University, he and his wife Katy live in Delaware, Ohio, where they raised their two daughters, Anne and Nora.

ACKNOWLEDGMENTS continued

Cornfield Review: "Anna Babb with Crow-Black Hair," "The Garden, the Children," "Kathleen Ni Houlihan," "Once You Learn You Never Forget," "Power";
Descant: "The Captain";
Hanging Loose: "Get Together";
Identity Theory: "Doc's Got the Blues," "Exchange Scholar," "Semper Fi";
Illinois Quarterly: "This Too a Matter of Degree";
The Little Magazine: "Indian Summer";
Midwest Quarterly: "At the Scene of a Car Train Collision," "For Birds";
Mill Mountain Review: "Birthday in the Mountains";
The New York Times: "Once My Father," "The Swimmer";
Northeast: "After Him";
Poetry Northwest: "On My Own Two Feet," "Whitman's Song";
River Run: "Knees";
The Shore Review: "Heroes";
Western Review: "Memories of an Obedient Childhood."

ANTHOLOGIES:
Doctor Generosity's Almanac, 1970, Generosity Press, New Jersey, edited by Ray Freed: "Cycle"
Heartland II, 1975, Northern Illinois University Press, edited by Lucien Stryk, "Atlas," "Heirloom"
73 Ohio Poets, 1980, Cornfield Review, Ohio State University, Marion, OH, edited by David Citino: "Power"
Walt Whitman: The Measure of His Song, 1981, Holy Cow Press, Duluth, MN, edited by Jim Perlman, Ed Folsom and Dan Campion, "Whitman's Song"
Poems 1978-83, 1983, Ohio Arts Council, Aid to Individual Artists Program, Columbus, OH, edited by Robert Fox: "Circus," "The Hearing of the Ear"
Poetry Ohio: the Art of the State, 1984, Ohio Arts Council, Columbus, OH, edited by Robert Fox: "Indian Summer"
An Introduction to Poetry, Seventh Edition, 1990, Harper Collins, NYC, edited by X.J. Kennedy: "Reply to an Eviction Notice
Literature: an Introduction to Fiction, Poetry and Drama, Fifth Edition, edited by X.J. Kennedy, Harper Collins, 1991: "Reply to an Eviction Notice"
Food Poems, Pocket Poems, 1996, Bottom Dog Press, Huron, OH, edited by David Lee Garrison and Terry Hermsen: "Fondue"
O Taste and See, 2003, Bottom Dog Press, Huron, OH, edited by David Lee Garrison and Terry Hermsen: "Fondue
Cap City Poets, 2008, Pudding House Publications, Columbus, OH, edited by Steve Abbott, Connie Willet Everett and Rose M. Smith: "Reply to an Eviction Notice"

CHAPBOOKS:

Not For Dietrich Bonhoeffer, 1969, New/Books, Trumansburg, N.Y. "After Him," "The Captain," "Pennsylvania Dutch Country," "Memories of an Obedient Childhood"

Body Home, 1971, Ulsterman Publications, Belfast, Northern Ireland: "Birthday in the Mountains," "Get Together," "Heat Lightning," "Heirloom," "Indian Summer"

At the Edge of the Ghost Town, 1972, Perkins Poets, The Bookshop, Leeds, England: "Picking Up Lindsay," "Window"

The Full Round, 1973, Fiddlehead Poetry Books, Fredericton, N.B., Canada: "At the Scene of a Car-Train Collision," "Beached," "Cycle," "The Open," "The Swimmer"

News From a Backward State, 1973, Northeast/Juniper Books, La Crosse, WI: "Coal Miner," "Heroes," "While I Was Driving," "News from a Backward State"

On My Own Two Feet, 1973, Fiddlehead Poetry Books, Fredericton, N.B., Canada: "Curse of the Werewolf," "Direction," "Dropping In," "Fondue," "Gloves," "On My Own Two Feet," "The West: Field Notes," "This Too a Matter of Degree," "Whitman's Song"

Once You Learn You Never Forget, 1978, Fiddlehead Poetry Books, Fredericton, N.B., Canada: "Circus," "The Garden the Children," "In Training a Man Talks to Himself," "Knees," "Once You Learn You Never Forget," "Reply to an Eviction Notice"

RECENT BOOKS BY BOTTOM DOG PRESS

BOTTOM DOG

PRESS

Reply to an Eviction Notice: Selected Poems by Robert Flanagan
978-1-933964-28-7   100 pgs. $15

Bar Stories edited by Nan Byrne
978-1-933964-09-6   168 pgs. $14

An Unmistakable Shade of Red & The Obama Chronicles
by Mary E. Weems
978-1-933964-18-8   80 pgs. $15

Cleveland Poetry Scenes: A Panorama and Anthology
eds. Nina Gibans, Mary Weems, Larry Smith
978-1933964-17-1   304 pgs. $20

d.a.levy & the mimeograph revolution
eds. Ingrid Swanberg & Larry Smith
1-933964-07-3 276 pgs. & dvd $25

Our Way of Life: Poems by Ray McNiece
978-1-933964-14-0   128 pgs. $14

Hunger Artist: Childhood in the Suburbs
by Joanne Jacobson
978-1-933964-11-9   132 pgs. $16

Come Together: Imagine Peace
eds. Ann Smith, Larry Smith, Philip Metres
978-1-933964-22-5   224 pgs. $18

Evensong: Contemporary American Poets on Spirituality
eds. Gerry LaFemina & Chad Prevost
ISBN 1-933964-01-4   276 pgs. $18

BOTTOM DOG PRESS
Order Online at: http://smithdocs.net

Recent Books by Bird Dog Publishing

Heart Murmurs: Poems by John Vanek
978-1-933964-27-0   120 pgs. $15

Faces and Voices: Tales by Larry Smith
1-933964-04-9   136 pgs. $14

Second Story Woman: A Memoir of Second Chances
by Carole Calladine
978-1-933964-12-6   226 pgs. $15

256 Zones of Gray: Poems
by Rob Smith
978-1-933964-16-4   80 pgs. $14

Another Life: Collected Poems by Allen Frost
978-1-933964-10-2   176 pgs. $14

Winter Apples: Poems by Paul S. Piper
978-1-933964-08-9   88 pgs. $14

Lake Effect: Poems by Laura Treacy Bentley
1-933964-05-7   108 pgs. $14

Depression Days on an Appalachian Farm: Poems
by Robert L. Tener
1-933964-03-0   80 pgs. $14

120 Charles Street, The Village:
Journals & Other Writings 1949-1950 by Holly Beye
0-933087-99-3   240 pgs. $15

Bird Dog Publishing
A division of Bottom Dog Press, Inc.
Order Online at: http://smithdocs.net/BirdDogy/BirdDogPage.html

Printed in the United States
217934BV00001B/2/P

9 781933 964287

With a fine gift for visual particulars, Flanagan make
us see his grandfather, the police captain's "eight bras
buttons." These intelligent, sharply focused poems recal
a gritty past of rented apartments, cracked tar, the figh
game, and turf wars in scenes of working class urban America
1950s. But this poet is also at ease with the natural worl
as he sinks his roots in the river beds of Ohio, dreamin
"peace for his children," flashing forward to insights o
a life lived through…I greet this strong and moving boo
with admiration and joy. It deserves a large and enthusiasti
audience.
                                                    —Colette Ine

What a wide slice of life Robert Flanagan's poems tak
in: knowing explorations of the "plowed heart of Ohio" an
other American places—memorable art made from familiar ex
perience. Flanagan wins me with his rich humor and compassior
his keen ear and sharp eye, his technical skill (se
"Memories of an Obedient Childhood"), his ability to sla
a poem shut with a crash ("The Hearing of the Ear"), hi
way with simile and metaphor ("Coal Miner"). Here is a rich
long overdue gathering of Flanagan's finest and most insight
ful poems, the harvest of four decades. Open this book an
you just might find it irresistible.
                                                    —X. J. Kenned

Robert Flanagan grew up in Toledo, Ohio
watching boxing with his father. He boxed
while in his teens—which eventually led t
a detached retina. He went on to Universit
of Toledo, where he discovered his love o
writing: poetry, fiction, plays, screenplays
and comedy routines. He honed his writing
skills at the University of Chicago. Flanagar
has since published a novel, three short
story collections, five chapbooks of poetry
essays and reviews, has had two stage plays and two screen
plays produced. Retired as director of creative writing at
Ohio Wesleyan University, he now lives in Delaware, Ohio

BOTTOM DOG PRESS

HURON, OHIO

ISBN 978-1-933964-28-7
90000
9 781933 964287

POETRY

WORKING LIVE
SERIES

$15.00